TH PRAYER GUIDE FOR THE REST OF US

MEDITATION IDEAS FOR THE HOLY ROSARY

Brent Villalobos

DEDICATION

To my wife, Barbara, who continuously reminds me of the importance of prayer and being connected to my Catholic faith. And to my boys, Luke and Peter, in the hope that I am doing my best guiding them in developing their faith

INTRODUCTION

Do you like to cook? I'm not much of a chef besides the occasional pancake brunch or grilled steak. But I have seen plenty of *Iron Chef* and other cooking shows and learned a few basic concepts. Mainly, I learned that simple ingredients can combine to form extremely nuanced and complex flavors. For example, a tomato may not seem like much on its own. But combine it with the right amount of olive oil, salt, butter, garlic, onion, and broth and you have a tasty soup.

In a way, the Rosary is much like a spiritual recipe made up of parts that are simple by themselves but, when combined, create a spiritually complex experience. It's the combination of prayers, meditations, and life experiences that make the Rosary such a rich and spiritually nutritious meal.

The foundation of the Rosary experience is the prayers themselves. They aren't difficult; a series of *Hail Marys* and *Our Fathers*. Most Catholics have been praying those since childhood and can say them without much effort. Many of us have said them so many times that it is easy to zoom through them and not give them much thought. But these are the important building blocks to the Rosary because they keep you grounded to something familiar. Unlike something dense like the Catechism or an encyclical which takes a lot of time and concentration to understand, the prayers of the Rosary are simple and accessible. But don't mistake simple for unimportant. Like salt, pepper, or oil, they are rather simple in nature but important to any recipe.

The mysteries are the next ingredient to this spiritual recipe. When you combine the prayers with the mysteries you start to create a deeper, meditative experience. You are no longer praying the *Hail Marys* and *Our Fathers* in a vacuum. You now have structure and direction. Each mystery reflects an aspect of our Christian faith that requires deeper scrutiny and thought. As you pray the *Hail Marys* in the Rosary, meditate on the current mystery. Ask Mary for help understanding what God wants you to take away from each mystery.

But there is yet another ingredient to consider. The final ingredient is you and the world you find yourself in. And this is where the Rosary takes on a complexity that makes it such a powerful prayer. The Rosary is never static because your life situation is always changing. You approach the Rosary with different concerns, sins, thanksgivings, and sorrows each time you pray it. It is you who brings out the true beauty and power of the Rosary.

Blending these core ingredients – prayer, mysteries, and life events, has been the goal of my website, RosaryMeds.com. I wanted to show people that the Rosary has a connection and a relevance to everything that happens in the world, either personally or to our society.

While RosaryMeds.com and my book, *The Rosary for the Rest of Us,* provide commentary on the Rosary in the form of resources and articles, I felt like I needed to write something to aid people through the Rosary praying experience itself. All the articles and books in the world don't mean much if you just draw blanks when you actually pray the Rosary. Or worse yet, the lack of meditation ideas discourages you from praying the Rosary at all.

I wrote this book in hope that providing Bible verses, intentions, and spiritually motivating quotations into a single prayer guide will provide an abundance of ideas for your Rosary meditations. Going back to the recipe analogy, think of this book as your idea cupboard which you can combine in many different ways depending on your circumstances.

The Rosary is grounded in Scripture and that is why I included Bible verses for each Rosary bead. Most of them are a single chapter taken from a Gospel telling the account of the mystery. And while you may have read or heard these chapters numerous times, I think you will continue to learn new lessons when you integrate them into Rosary prayer. This goes back to the idea that you bring different life experiences each time you pray the Rosary and hence, the Bible will reveal different insights each time you read and meditate on it.

I also thought that including quotations from saints and theologians would provide a needed boost of motivation. When our passion for Rosary prayer or practicing our faith begins to wane, we often need a small kick to renew our zeal. Like a coach delivering a motivational speech to his players, we need to periodically hear why praying the Rosary with passion is so important. Personally, I felt more motivated to pray the Rosary every time I found yet another quotation touting the Rosary's many benefits while writing this book. I hope you are similarly motivated reading and contemplating them.

Intentions are also another important aspect to Rosary prayer. This brings the prayers out a spiritual vacuum and again into our dynamic, always-changing lives. Despite our best intentions, we forget all of those who are in need of our prayers and actions. Having an intention per Rosary bead reminds us of all the people who need, not just our prayers, but also our help.

There really is no correct way to use this guide. Feel free to read the Scripture verse, intention, and quotation before praying a *Hail Mary* or mix and match however you want. Maybe one day you just read the Bible verses and pray solely a scriptural Rosary. Another day you might focus solely on intentions. It's up to you to find whatever pattern works best. The important goal is that you find the pattern that keeps you returning to the Rosary day after day.

Remember, a Rosary a day keeps the devil away!

ROSARY BASICS

Most rosaries look like a necklace (but it is not a piece of jewelry!). The first section is outside the main loop and includes the crucifix, one bead, three small beads, and another separate bead. On the crucifix, you pray the *Apostles' Creed*. On the single bead next to the crucifix you pray the *Lord's Prayer* (commonly known as the *Our Father*). On each of the three smaller beads you pray a *Hail Mary*. These three *Hail Mary* prayers are for the virtues of increased faith, hope, and charity. Finally, you pray the *Glory Be*. The *Glory Be* does not have a bead. The last bead on the chain is where you begin praying the first of the five decades.

Physically, each decade is represented on a Rosary by a separated bead followed by ten joined beads. Again, the separated bead for the first decade is actually not in the loop but is the last bead on the chain outside the main loop. On the single, separated bead you pray the *Our Father*. On each of the ten joined beads, you pray a *Hail Mary*. At the end of each decade, you pray a *Glory Be* and the *Fatima Prayer*.

Note that there is no bead for those last two prayers. Many people choose to either remain holding the tenth bead of the decade or grasp that gap between that tenth bead and the one for the *Our Father* of the next decade.

After the fifth decade, you pray the *Hail, Holy Queen*. Many people hold that large bead or emblem of the Virgin Mary that connects the crucifix chain to the main loop. Finally, feel free to pray any extra prayers before finishing. Common prayers include the *Rosary Prayer*, the *Prayer to St. Michael*, *Prayer for the Souls in Purgatory*, and any extra intentions you want to present to God.

There are 20 mysteries of the Rosary divided into four groups, or chaplets, that follow different aspects of Jesus' life. Each chaplet of mysteries has five decades where each decade (ten joined beads and one separate bead) represents one mystery. When you pray the Rosary, you typically focus on a specific set of mysteries. The mystery sets and their basic themes are:

- Joyful Mysteries – Jesus' birth and early childhood
- Luminous Mysteries – Jesus' ministry
- Sorrowful Mysteries – Jesus' Passion and death
- Glorious Mysteries – Jesus' Resurrection

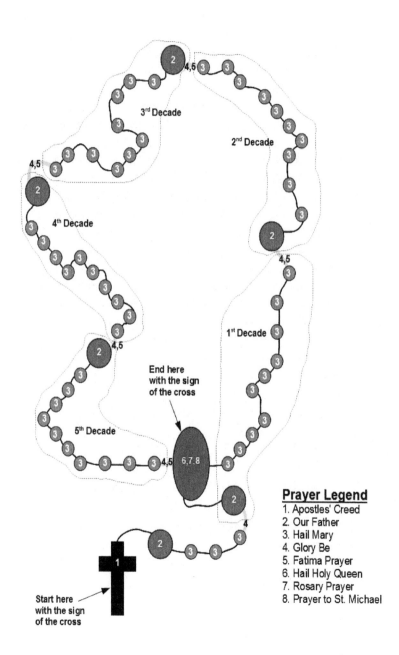

2

3 3

3rd Decade

2 4,5 3 3

3 3

3 3

3 2nd Decade

3 3

3 3 3

3 3

4,5 3

3 2

3 3

2 4,5

4th Decade

3

3 3

3 1st Decade 3

3 3

3 3

3 3

3

3 3

2 4,5 End here
with the sign
of the cross

3 3

3 5th Decade 3 3 3 4,5 6,7,8 3 3

2

4

1

2 3 3 3

Start here
with the sign
of the cross

Prayer Legend
1. Apostles' Creed
2. Our Father
3. Hail Mary
4. Glory Be
5. Fatima Prayer
6. Hail Holy Queen
7. Rosary Prayer
8. Prayer to St. Michael

There is a schedule for what day to pray each set of mysteries. However, it is fine to change the order or pray more than one set of mysteries on a given day. For example, perhaps you are going through a difficult time in your life and so you might want to pray the Sorrowful Mysteries more often to gather more strength. This is the schedule that Blessed Pope John Paul II suggested:

- Monday – Joyful Mysteries
- Tuesday – Sorrowful Mysteries
- Wednesday – Glorious Mysteries
- Thursday – Luminous Mysteries
- Friday – Sorrowful Mysteries
- Saturday – Joyful Mysteries
- Sunday – Glorious Mysteries (exceptions are praying the Joyful Mysteries during the Christmas season and the Sorrowful Mysteries during Lent)

The Joyful Mysteries

The Annunciation

The Visitation

The Nativity

The Presentation

The Finding in the Temple

The First Joyful Mystery
The Annunciation

Lord, I ask You for the courage to follow Your Will no matter how challenging it may seem. Like Mary, I want to put my faith in Your divine plan because it ultimately leads me to Your heavenly kingdom.

Our Father

In the sixth month, the angel Gabriel was sent from God to a town of Galilee called Nazareth, to a virgin betrothed to a man named Joseph, of the house of David, and the virgin's name was Mary. (Luke 1:26-27)

Mother Mary, please guide those who are contemplating their life's vocation.

"Have you strayed from the path leading to heaven? Then call on Mary, for Her name means "Star of the Sea, the North Star which guides the ships of our souls during the voyage of this life," and She will guide you to the harbor of eternal salvation." – St. Louis de Montfort

Hail Mary

And coming to Her, he said, "Hail, favored one! The Lord is with You." (Luke 1:28)

Mother Mary, I pray for increased faith in God's plan for me even when confronted with difficulties and disappointments.

"Whoever shall faithfully serve me by the recitation of the Rosary, shall receive signal graces."
– Our Lady's promise to St. Dominic

Hail Mary

But She was greatly troubled at what was said and pondered what sort of greeting this might be. (Luke 1:29)

Mother Mary, I pray for expecting mothers, especially those with unplanned pregnancies (like Yours) and those who are scared of their future.

"The works of Jesus and Mary can also be called wonderful flowers; but their perfume and beauty can only be appreciated by those who study them carefully —and who open them and drink in their scent by diligent and sincere meditation." – St. Louis de Montfort

Hail Mary

Then the angel said to Her, "Do not be afraid, Mary, for You have found favor with God." (Luke 1:30)

Mother Mary, I pray for those who are scared about what God has planned for them; that they find the strength to believe in the goodness of His plans.

"I promise my special protection and the greatest graces to all those who shall recite the Rosary."
– Our Lady's promise to St. Dominic

Hail Mary

"Behold, You will conceive in Your womb and bear a son, and You shall name him Jesus." (Luke 1:30)

Mother Mary, I ask You to instill in me a sense of joy when I follow the path God sets before me.

"Three steps to climb to go to God: the first, which is the nearest to us, and the most suited to our capacity, is Mary; the second is Jesus Christ; and the third is God the Father. To go to Jesus, we must go to Mary; She is our mediatrix of intercession." – St. Louis de Montfort

Hail Mary

"He will be great and will be called Son of the Most High, and the Lord God will give Him the throne of David His father." (Luke 1:31)

Mother Mary, remind me that God never gives me a challenge I cannot handle (especially with Your intercession).

"Mary has produced, together with the Holy Ghost, the greatest thing which has been or ever will be—a God-Man; and She will consequently produce the greatest saints that there will be in the end of time."
– St. Louis de Montfort

Hail Mary

"And He will rule over the house of Jacob forever, and of His kingdom there will be no end." (Luke 1:31)

Lord, save me from the temptation of taking a seemingly easier path in life that doesn't bring me closer to God's grace.

"Just as Mary excels in all other perfections, She surpasses us all in the virtue of gratitude; so She would never let us honor Her with love and respect without repaying us one hundred fold." – St. Louis de Montfort

Hail Mary

But Mary said to the angel, "How can this be, since I have no relations with a man?" (Luke 1:34)

Mother Mary, lovingly nudge those who have swayed from God's path back to His truth.

"The Rosary shall be a powerful armor against hell, it will destroy vice, decrease sin, and defeat heresies." – Our Lady's promise to St. Dominic

Hail Mary

And the angel said to Her in reply, "The Holy Spirit will come upon You, and the power of the Most High will overshadow You. Therefore the child to be born will be called holy, the Son of God." (Luke 1:35)

Mother Mary, guide parents everywhere to lead their children closer to God's grace through prayer, education, and as an example of living the faith.

"Saint Dominic has divided up the lives of Our Lord and Our Lady into fifteen mysteries which stand for their virtues and their most important actions. These are the fifteen tableaux; or pictures whose every detail must rule and inspire our lives." – St. Louis de Montfort

Hail Mary

Mary said, "Behold, I am the handmaid of the Lord. May it be done to me according to Your word."
(Luke 1:38)

Mother Mary, guide priests and nuns to faithfully live their often difficult vocations.

"The Rosary will cause virtue and good works to flourish; it will obtain for souls the abundant mercy of God; it will withdraw the heart of men from the love of the world and its vanities, and will lift them to the desire of eternal things. Oh, that souls would sanctify themselves by this means."
– Our Lady's promise to St. Dominic

Hail Mary

Glory Be

Oh My Jesus (Fatima Prayer)

The Second Joyful Mystery
The Visitation

Lord, You have given each of us unique and powerful talents. May we recognize our God-given abilities and go out into the world doing Your Will as Mary did when She visited Her cousin, Elizabeth.

Our Father

During those days Mary set out and traveled to the hill country in haste to a town of Judah, where She entered the house of Zechariah and greeted Elizabeth.
(Luke 1:39-40)

Mother Mary, I pray for the motivation to go out and do God's will as You did when You visited and helped Elizabeth.

"The soul which recommends itself to me by the recitation of the Rosary shall not perish."
– Our Lady's promise to St. Dominic

Hail Mary

When Elizabeth heard Mary's greeting, the infant leaped in her womb, and Elizabeth, filled with the Holy Spirit, cried out in a loud voice and said, "Most blessed are You among women, and blessed is the fruit of Your womb." (Luke 1:41-42)

Mother Mary, I pray that pregnant women who carry a precious life find the spiritual, physical, and emotional strength like You and Elizabeth.

"The name Mary which means 'lady of light' shows that God has filled me with wisdom and light, like a shining star, to light up Heaven and earth."
– St. Louis de Montfort

Hail Mary

"And how does this happen to me, that the mother of my Lord should come to me? For at the moment the sound of Your greeting reached my ears, the infant in my womb leaped for joy." (Luke 1:43-44)

Mother Mary, I pray for mercy and the conversion for those who seek to harm the most innocent among us.

"The words *full of grace* remind me that the Holy Spirit has showered so many graces upon me that I am able to give these graces in abundance to those who ask for them through me as Mediatrix."
– St. Louis de Montfort

Hail Mary

"Blessed are You who believed that what was spoken to You by the Lord would be fulfilled." (Luke 1:45)

Mother Mary, I pray for faith to follow God's plan, wherever it leads me in life.

"When people say 'The Lord is with thee,' they renew the indescribable joy that was mine when the Eternal Word became incarnate in my [Mary's] womb."
– St. Louis de Montfort

Hail Mary

And Mary said, "My soul proclaims the greatness of the Lord; my spirit rejoices in God my savior."
(Luke 1:46-47)

Mother Mary, I pray for the yearning to serve others rather than be served.

"When you say to me [Mary] blessed art thou among women I praise Almighty God's Divine mercy which lifted me to this exalted plane of happiness."
– St. Louis de Montfort

Hail Mary

"For He has looked upon His handmaid's lowliness; behold, from now on will all ages call me blessed."
(Luke 1:48)

Mother Mary, I pray that I follow up with action what I learn from God through prayer.

"And at the words blessed is the fruit of thy womb, Jesus, the whole of Heaven rejoices with me [Mary] to see my Son Jesus Christ adored and glorified for having saved mankind." – St. Louis de Montfort

Hail Mary

"The Mighty One has done great things for me, and holy is His name. His mercy is from age to age to those who fear Him." (Luke 1:49-50)

Mother Mary, I pray for those who hear God's call but are afraid to act on it; that they receive the motivation they need.

"Whoever shall recite the Rosary devoutly, applying himself to the consideration of its sacred mysteries, shall never be conquered and never overwhelmed by misfortune. God will not chastise him in His justice, he shall not perish by an unprovided death (unprepared for heaven). The sinner shall convert. The just shall grow in grace and become worthy of eternal life."
– Our Lady's promise to St. Dominic

Hail Mary

"He has shown might with His arm, dispersed the arrogant of mind and heart." (Luke 1:51)

Mother Mary, I pray that I am a public advocate for life at all stages.

"Whoever shall have a true devotion for the Rosary shall not die without the sacraments of the Church."
– Our Lady's promise to St. Dominic

Hail Mary

"He has thrown down the rulers from their thrones but lifted up the lowly. The hungry He has filled with good things; the rich He has sent away empty."
(Luke 1:52-53)

Mother Mary, I ask You to ease my fear of being a visible and public witness of the Catholic faith in this often hostile world.

"To say the Holy Rosary to advantage one must be in a state of grace or at the very least be fully determined to give up mortal sin." – St. Louis de Montfort

Hail Mary

"He has helped Israel His servant, remembering His mercy, according to His promise to our fathers, to Abraham and to His descendants forever."
(Luke 1:54-55)

Mother Mary, I pray that I show charity, not only financially, but also through exercising my talents.

"Those who are faithful to recite the Rosary shall have, during their life and at their death, the light of God and the plenitude of His graces; at the moment of death they shall participate in the merits of the saints in paradise." – Our Lady's promise to St. Dominic

Hail Mary

Glory Be

Oh My Jesus (Fatima Prayer)

The Third Joyful Mystery
The Nativity

Lord, You came into this world in a most unexpected way. May I always look for You in prayer and see You acting in my life even when it is in ways I do not expect.

Our Father

And Joseph too went up from Galilee from the town of Nazareth to Judea, to the city of David that is called Bethlehem, because he was of the house and family of David, to be enrolled with Mary, his betrothed, who was with child. (Luke 2:4-5)

Mother Mary, show me the humility that allows God to be born into my heart.

"To pray well, it is not enough to give expression to our petitions by means of that most excellent of all prayers, the Rosary, but we must also pray with real concentration for God listens more to the voice of the heart than that of the mouth." – St. Louis de Montfort

Hail Mary

While they were there, the time came for Her to have Her child, and She gave birth to Her firstborn son. She wrapped Him in swaddling clothes and laid Him in a manger, because there was no room for them in the inn. (Luke 2:5-7)

Mother Mary, I pray that I accept that God's ways are not always my ways but that they do lead me to ultimate happiness.

"To be guilty of willful distractions during prayer would show a great lack of respect and reverence; it would make our Rosaries fruitless and would make us guilty of sin." – St. Louis de Montfort

Hail Mary

Now there were shepherds in that region living in the fields and keeping the night watch over their flock. The angel of the Lord appeared to them and the glory of the Lord shone around them, and they were struck with great fear. (Luke 2:8-9)

Mother Mary, I pray that I follow the signs to Jesus like the wise men and the shepherds at His birth.

"How can we expect God to listen to us if we ourselves do not pay attention to what we are saying? How can we expect Him to be pleased if, while in the presence of His tremendous Majesty, we give in to distractions just as children run after butterflies?"
– St. Louis de Montfort

Hail Mary

The angel said to them, "Do not be afraid; for behold, I proclaim to you good news of great joy that will be for all the people." (Luke 2:10)

Mother Mary, I pray that I can rejoice in God who so loved me that He humbled himself and took human form in the person of Jesus.

"Among Catholics those who bear the mark of God's reprobation think but little of the Rosary (whether that of five decades or fifteen). They either fail to say it or only say it very quickly and in a lukewarm manner."
– St. Louis de Montfort

Hail Mary

"For today in the city of David a savior has been born for you who is Messiah and Lord." (Luke 2:11)

Mother Mary, I pray that I see Jesus in everyone, even my enemies.

"I shall deliver from purgatory those who have been devoted to the Rosary."
– Our Lady's promise to St. Dominic

Hail Mary

So they went in haste and found Mary and Joseph, and the infant lying in the manger. (Luke 2:16)

Mother Mary, I pray that like the shepherds in the fields, I make time to be with Jesus through prayer.

"The faithful children of the Rosary shall merit a high degree of glory in heaven."
– Our Lady's promise to St. Dominic

Hail Mary

When they saw this, they made known the message that had been told them about this child. (Luke 2:17)

Mother Mary, I pray for forgiveness for the times I rejected God's plan for me.

"All the gifts, virtues and graces of the Holy Ghost are distributed by Mary, to whom She wishes, when She wishes, the way She wishes, and as much as She wishes."
– St. Louis de Montfort

Hail Mary

All who heard it were amazed by what had been told them by the shepherds. (Luke 2:18)

Mother Mary, I pray for forgiveness for the times I have not seen Jesus in my brothers and sisters.

"You shall obtain all you ask of me by the recitation of the Rosary." – Our Lady's promise to St. Dominic

Hail Mary

And Mary kept all these things, reflecting on them in Her heart. (Luke 2:19)

Mother Mary, I pray that I am open to God's message even when it comes in unexpected ways.

"All those who propagate the holy Rosary shall be aided by me in their necessities."
– Our Lady's promise to St. Dominic

Hail Mary

Then the shepherds returned, glorifying and praising God for all they had heard and seen, just as it had been told to them. (Luke 2:20)

Mother Mary, I pray that I make an effort to attend adoration of the Blessed Sacrament.

"I have obtained from my Divine Son that all the advocates of the Rosary shall have for intercessors the entire celestial court during their life and at the hour of death." – Our Lady's promise to St. Dominic

Hail Mary

Glory Be

Oh My Jesus (Fatima Prayer)

The Fourth Joyful Mystery
The Presentation

Lord, fill my heart with a longing to act devoutly and righteously by devoting myself to a life of active prayer. May I have the faith and hope in the many promises You have made to me and the Catholic Church.

Our Father

When the days were completed for their purification according to the law of Moses, they took Him up to Jerusalem to present Him to the Lord, (Luke 2:22)

Mother Mary, I pray that I have faith, like Saint Simeon, that God's promises to me will always be fulfilled.

"All who recite the Rosary are my sons, and brothers of my only son Jesus Christ."
– Our Lady's promise to St. Dominic

Hail Mary

Just as it is written in the law of the Lord, "Every male that opens the womb shall be consecrated to the Lord," (Luke 2:23)

Mother Mary, I pray that I have the patience for God's plan for me to manifest itself.

"Devotion of my Rosary is a great sign of predestination." – Our Lady's promise to St. Dominic

Hail Mary

And to offer the sacrifice of "a pair of turtledoves or two young pigeons," in accordance with the dictate in the law of the Lord. (Luke 2:24)

Mother Mary, I pray that I continue to pray regularly even when I doubt God hears and answers me.

"The greatest saints, those richest in grace and virtue will be the most assiduous in praying to the most Blessed Virgin, looking up to Her as the perfect model to imitate and as a powerful helper to assist them."
– St. Louis de Montfort

Hail Mary

Now there was a man in Jerusalem whose name was Simeon. This man was righteous and devout, awaiting the consolation of Israel, and the Holy Spirit was upon him. (Luke 2:25)

Mother Mary, I pray for those who do not practice their faith out of discouragement because they don't think God hears them.

"Men do not fear a powerful hostile army as the powers of hell fear the name and protection of Mary."
– St. Bonaventure

Hail Mary

It had been revealed to him by the Holy Spirit that he should not see death before he had seen the Messiah of the Lord. (Luke 2:26)

Mother Mary, I pray that I always live faithfully to Catholic teachings even when it's difficult to do so.

"O sinner, be not discouraged, but have recourse to Mary in all your necessities. Call Her to your assistance, for such is the divine Will that She should help in every kind of necessity."
– St. Basil the Great

Hail Mary

He came in the Spirit into the temple; and when the parents brought in the child Jesus to perform the custom of the law in regard to him, (Luke 2:27)

Mother Mary, I pray for the forgiveness and conversion of those in society who mock or persecute the faithful.

"If you invoke the Blessed Virgin when you are tempted, She will come at once to your help, and Satan will leave you." – St. John Vianney

Hail Mary

He took Him into his arms and blessed God, saying: "Now, Master, You may let Your servant go in peace, according to Your word, for my eyes have seen Your salvation, which You prepared in sight of all the peoples, a light for revelation to the Gentiles, and glory for Your people Israel." (Luke 2:28-32)

Mother Mary, I pray that families can imitate the spirit and faith of the Holy Family.

"If you ever feel distressed during your day — call upon our Lady — just say this simple prayer: 'Mary, Mother of Jesus, please be a mother to me now.' I must admit — this prayer has never failed me."
– St. Mother Teresa

Hail Mary

The child's father and mother were amazed at what was said about Him; (Luke 2:33)

Mother Mary, I pray for those who have a broken family life, that they look to the Holy Family for guidance.

"All the sins of your life seem to be rising up against you. Don't give up hope! On the contrary, call your holy mother Mary, with the faith and abandonment of a child. She will bring peace to your soul."
– St. Josemaria Escriva

Hail Mary

And Simeon blessed them and said to Mary his mother, "Behold, this child is destined for the fall and rise of many in Israel," (Luke 2:34)

Mother Mary, I pray for those who are new parents; that they educate their children to actively practice their faith.

"When you see the storm coming, if you seek safety in that firm refuge which is Mary, there will be no danger of you wavering or going down."
– St. Josemaria Escriva

Hail Mary

"And to be a sign that will be contradicted (and you yourself a sword will pierce) so that the thoughts of many hearts may be revealed." (Luke 2:34-35)

Mother Mary, I pray for the elderly and dying; that they may go peacefully into God's kingdom.

"No one will ever be the servant of the Son without serving the Mother."
– St. Ildephonsus, Bishop

Hail Mary

Glory Be

Oh My Jesus (Fatima Prayer)

The Fifth Joyful Mystery
The Finding in the Temple

Lord, may I always look for You in my prayers, actions, words, and thoughts. May everything I do be in an effort to move into a deeper communion and friendship with You. May the thought of losing Your grace strengthen me in resisting the temptation to sin.

Our Father

Each year His parents went to Jerusalem for the feast of Passover, and when He was twelve years old, they went up according to festival custom. (Luke 2:41-42)

Mother Mary, I pray that I make the time to periodically examine my conscience in prayer.

"God the Father made an assemblage of all the waters and He named it the sea (mare). He made an assemblage of all His graces and He called it Mary (Maria)." – St. Louis de Montfort

Hail Mary

After they had completed its days, as they were returning, the boy Jesus remained behind in Jerusalem, but His parents did not know it. (Luke 2:43)

Mother Mary, I pray that I make time to regularly receive the Sacrament of Reconciliation and resolve not to commit the same sins again.

"We may seek graces, but shall never find them without the intercession of Mary." – St. Cajetan

Hail Mary

Thinking that He was in the caravan, they journeyed for a day and looked for Him among their relatives and acquaintances, but not finding Him, they returned to Jerusalem to look for Him. (Luke 2:44-45)

Mother Mary, I pray that I have the strength to make adjustments in my life to better live according to God's will.

"All true children of God have God for their father and Mary for his mother; anyone who does not have Mary for his mother, does not have God for his father."
– St. Louis de Montfort

Hail Mary

After three days they found Him in the temple, sitting in the midst of the teachers, listening to them and asking them questions, (Luke 2:46)

Mother Mary, I pray for the return of those who have wandered far from God's grace.

"It is by Her [Mary] that He [God] applies His merits to His members, and that He communicates His virtues, and distributes His graces."
– St. Louis de Montfort

Hail Mary

And all who heard Him were astounded at His understanding and His answers. (Luke 2:47)

Mother Mary, I pray for those who are undertaking the difficult path of redemptive suffering for their sins.

"She [Mary] is His [God] mysterious canal; She is His aqueduct, through which He makes His mercies flow gently and abundantly." – St. Louis de Montfort

Hail Mary

When His parents saw Him, they were astonished, and His mother said to Him, "Son, why have You done this to us?" (Luke 2:48)

Mother Mary, I pray that I listen to God's truth no matter who it is from.

"The greatest saints, those richest in grace and virtue will be the most assiduous in praying to the most Blessed Virgin, looking up to Her as the perfect model to imitate and as a powerful helper to assist them."
– St. Louis de Montfort

Hail Mary

"Your father and I have been looking for You with great anxiety." (Luke 2:48)

Mother Mary, I pray that our Church leaders follow and faithfully exercise the teachings of Jesus Christ.

"Always stay close to this Heavenly Mother, because She is the sea to be crossed to reach the shores of Eternal Splendor." – St. Padre Pio

Hail Mary

And He said to them, "Why were you looking for me? Did you not know that I must be in my Father's house?" (Luke 2:49)

Mother Mary, I pray for those who have not gone to confession in a long time, that they may find the courage and humility to become fully united with God through the Sacrament of Reconciliation.

"You are My Mother, the Mother of Mercy, and the consolation of the souls in Purgatory."
– St. Bridget to Our Lady

Hail Mary

But they did not understand what He said to them. He went down with them and came to Nazareth, and was obedient to them; (Luke 2:50-51)

Mother Mary, I pray that I look towards my local parish community as a way of finding Jesus in "His father's house."

"In trial or difficulty, I have recourse to Mother Mary, whose glance alone is enough to dissipate every fear."
– St. Therese of Lisieux

Hail Mary

And His mother kept all these things in Her heart. And Jesus advanced [in] wisdom and age and favor before God and man. (Luke 2:51-52)

Mother Mary, I pray that I imitate Jesus' obedience to God by obeying the precepts of the Catholic faith.

"Let us run to Her, and, as Her little children, cast ourselves into Her arms with a perfect confidence." – St. Francis de Sales

Hail Mary

Glory Be

Oh My Jesus (Fatima Prayer)

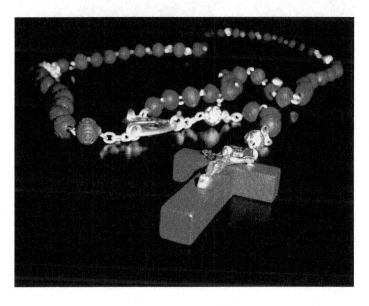

The Luminous Mysteries

Jesus' Baptism in the River
Jordan

The Miracle at Cana

The Proclamation of the
Kingdom of Heaven and the Call
to Conversion

The Transfiguration

The Institution of the Eucharist

The First Luminous Mystery
Jesus' Baptism in the River Jordan

Lord, may I remember my baptismal vows to love and honor You in everything I do. Lord, may I listen to the call to repentance from all those who follow in the steps of John the Baptist.

Our Father

Then people from Jerusalem, all of Judea, and all the region around the Jordan went out to him. (Matthew 3:5)

Holy Mother, help me heed God's commands and listen to Jesus' teachings.

"Moral principles do not depend on a majority vote."
– Ven. Archbishop Fulton John Sheen

Hail Mary

They were baptized by him in the Jordan, confessing their sins. (Matthew 3:6)

Holy Mother, help me strive to be as sinless and innocent as I was at my baptism.

"The liturgy is not about you and I... The liturgy is first and foremost about God and what He has done for us." – Cardinal Robert Sarah

Hail Mary

"I indeed baptize you with water for repentance." But he who is coming after me is mightier than I, whose sandals I am not worthy to bear." (Matthew 3:11)

Holy Mother, I pray for those who have forgotten their baptismal promises; that the Holy Spirit guides them back to their faith.

"If one were to consider how much Jesus suffered, one would not commit the smallest sin."
– St. Gianna Beretta Molla

Hail Mary

"He will baptize you with the Holy Spirit and fire."
(Matthew 3:11)

Holy Mother, I pray for godparents, that they continue to pray for and guide their godchildren in developing their faith.

"Say the holy Rosary. Blessed be that monotony of Hail Mary's which purifies the monotony of your sins!" – St. Josemaria Escriva

Hail Mary

Then Jesus came from Galilee to John at the Jordan to be baptized by him. (Matthew 3:13)

Holy Mother, I pray for parents, that they continue to lead their children in practicing their faith by setting a good example.

"Those who pray, have hope. Those who pray little, are in great danger. Those who do not pray, are lost."
– St Padre Pio

Hail Mary

John tried to prevent Him, saying, "I need to be baptized by You, and yet You are coming to me?" (Matthew 3:14)

Holy Mother, I pray to God for forgiveness for the times I have not listened to Jesus as I vowed in my baptism.

"The refusal to take sides on great moral issues is itself a decision. It is a silent acquiescence to evil."
– Ven. Archbishop Fulton John Sheen

Hail Mary

Jesus said to him in reply, "Allow it now, for thus it is fitting for us to fulfill all righteousness." Then He allowed him. (Matthew 3:15)

Holy Mother, I pray that I may be a living reminder to others about the joy of the Catholic faith.

"The tragedy of our time is that those who still believe in honesty lack fire and conviction, while those who believe in dishonesty are full of passionate conviction." – Ven. Archbishop Fulton John Sheen

Hail Mary

After Jesus was baptized, He came up from the water and behold, the heavens were opened [for Him], (Matthew 3:16)

Holy Mother, I pray for those who have not been baptized, that they live morally according to God's natural law imprinted on their hearts.

"Do you want our Lord to give you many graces? Visit Him often." – St. John Bosco

Hail Mary

And He saw the Spirit of God descending like a dove [and] coming upon Him. (Matthew 3:16)

Holy Mother, I pray for the conversion of those living contrary to God's plan for them.

"He did not say you would not be troubled. You would not be tempted. You would not be distressed. But He did say you would not be overcome."
– St. Josemaria Escriva

Hail Mary

And a voice came from the heavens, saying, "This is my beloved Son, with whom I am well pleased." (Matthew 3:17)

Holy Mother, I pray that I listen to the Holy Spirit who is always guiding me towards the grace promised to me through my baptism.

"Never be afraid of loving the Blessed Virgin too much. You can never love Her more than Jesus did."
– St. Maximilian Kolbe

Hail Mary

Glory Be

Oh My Jesus (Fatima Prayer)

The Second Luminous Mystery
The Miracle at Cana

Lord, may Your miracles come upon those who truly need them so that we may all increase our faith in You. May I not ask for miracles to suit my worldly desires but instead see Your miracles as signs of Your presence in my life.

Our Father

On the third day, there was a wedding in Cana in Galilee, and the mother of Jesus was there. (John 2:1)

Holy Mother, I pray that those who need God's miracles the most receive them.

"The greatest method of praying is to pray the Rosary." – St. Francis de Sales

Hail Mary

Jesus and His disciples were also invited to the wedding. (John 2:2)

Holy Mother, help me see how I can serve others and be a miracle to them.

"When the Holy Rosary is said well, it gives Jesus and Mary more glory and is more meritorious than any other prayer." – St. Louis de Montfort

Hail Mary

When the wine ran short, the mother of Jesus said to Him, "They have no wine." (John 2:3)

Holy Mother, I pray that I do not ask for miracles for my selfish desires but instead see them as God's tool for increasing my faith.

"The Holy Rosary is the storehouse of countless blessing." – Blessed Alan de la Roche

Hail Mary

[And] Jesus said to Her, "Woman, how does Your concern affect me? My hour has not yet come." (John 2:4)

Holy Mother, I pray for a spiritual awakening of those who do not believe in God's awesome power.

"One day, through the Rosary and the Scapular, Our Lady will save the world." – St. Dominic

Hail Mary

His mother said to the servers, "Do whatever He tells you." (John 2:5)

Holy Mother, I pray for those who question their faith because they don't understand why they do not receive the miracles they request.

"If you say the Rosary faithfully unto death, I do assure you that, in spite of the gravity of your sins, 'you will receive a never-fading crown of glory'."
– St. Louis de Montfort

Hail Mary

Now there were six stone water jars there for Jewish ceremonial washings, each holding twenty to thirty gallons. (John 2:6)

Holy Mother, I pray that I may see and give glory to God for all the small miracles that surround me.

"If there were one million families praying the Rosary every day, the entire world would be saved."
– St. Pope Pius X

Hail Mary

Jesus told them, "Fill the jars with water." So they filled them to the brim. (John 2:7)

Holy Mother, I pray that like the servers at the wedding, I listen to Your guidance to do whatever Jesus tells me.

"Recite your Rosary with faith, with humility, with confidence, and with perseverance."
– St. Louis de Montfort

Hail Mary

Then He told them, "Draw some out now and take it to the headwaiter." So they took it. (John 2:8)

Holy Mother, I pray for those who live in sin; for their conversion and that they strive to live the remainder of their lives giving their very best to God.

"The holy Rosary is a powerful weapon. Use it with confidence and you'll be amazed at the results."
– St. Josemaria Escriva

Hail Mary

And when the headwaiter tasted the water that had become wine, without knowing where it came from (although the servers who had drawn the water knew), the headwaiter called the bridegroom and said to him, "Everyone serves good wine first, and then when people have drunk freely, an inferior one; but you have kept the good wine until now." (John 2:9-10)

Holy Mother, I pray for those who live in misery, that they know that God has saved the "best for last" which is eternal joy in Heaven.

"You always leave the Rosary for later, and you end up not saying it at all because you are sleepy. If there is no other time, say it in the street without letting anybody notice it. It will, moreover, help you to have presence of God." – St. Josemaria Escriva

Hail Mary

Jesus did this as the beginning of His signs in Cana in Galilee and so revealed His glory, and His disciples began to believe in Him. (John 2:11)

Holy Mother, help me place my faith in Jesus for the seemingly small events in my life, not just the large ones.

"There is no problem, I tell you, no matter how difficult it is, that we cannot solve by the prayer of the Holy Rosary." – Sister Lucia dos Santos, Fatima seer

Hail Mary

Glory Be

Oh My Jesus (Fatima Prayer)

The Third Luminous Mystery
The Proclamation of the Kingdom of Heaven and the Call for Conversion

Lord, may I live in a constant state of conversion; always looking for ways I can better live according to Your teachings. Forgive me for the times I have focused more on worldly desires rather than the true happiness of Your Kingdom of Heaven.

Our Father

Jesus returned to Galilee in the power of the Spirit, and news of Him spread throughout the whole region.
(Luke 4:14)

Holy Mother, I pray that I lead a life of conversion towards God's truth.

"Those who meditate on my Seven Sorrows will be protected by me at every instance of their life."
– Our Mother Mary

Hail Mary

He taught in their synagogues and was praised by all.
(Luke 4:15)

Holy Mother, help me put the goal of living in the Kingdom of Heaven in front of my earthly desires.

"May the Rosary never fall from your hands."
– St. Pope John XXIII

Hail Mary

He came to Nazareth, where He had grown up, and went according to His custom into the synagogue on the sabbath day. (Luke 4:16)

Holy Mother, I pray for mercy on those who put their worldly desires above all else.

"Jesus permits the spiritual combat as a purification, not as a punishment." – St. Padre Pio

Hail Mary

He stood up to read and was handed a scroll of the prophet Isaiah. (Luke 4:17)

Holy Mother, I pray that I may help proclaim the joys of the Kingdom of Heaven to others.

"A soul that trusts God is invincible." – Mother Angelica

Hail Mary

He unrolled the scroll and found the passage where it was written: "The Spirit of the Lord is upon me, because He has anointed me to bring glad tidings to the poor. (Luke 4:17-18)

Holy Mother, help me actively assist others convert their worldly ways to God's ways.

"What people don't realize is how much religion costs. They think faith is a big electric blanket, when of course it is the cross." – Flannery O'Connor

Hail Mary

He has sent me to proclaim liberty to captives and recovery of sight to the blind, to let the oppressed go free, and to proclaim a year acceptable to the Lord." (Luke 4:19)

Holy Mother, I pray that I do not reject Jesus' teachings no matter how difficult or far-fetched they may seem.

"One of the first things the devil always does is to make people stop praying." – St. Jean Vianney

Hail Mary

Rolling up the scroll, He handed it back to the attendant and sat down, and the eyes of all in the synagogue looked intently at Him. (Luke 4:20)

Holy Mother, give me the strength to live my faith even when others may persecute me for it.

"Coincidence is God's way of remaining anonymous." – Albert Einstein

Hail Mary

He said to them, "Today this scripture passage is fulfilled in your hearing." (Luke 4:21)

Holy Mother, I pray that I make the time to read the Bible and learn about God's Kingdom as Jesus taught.

"I see Mary everywhere, I see difficulties nowhere."
– St. Maximilian Kolbe

Hail Mary

"Unless a man be born of water and the Spirit, he cannot enter the kingdom of God." (John 3:5)

Holy Mother, help me let go of whatever distracts me from following Jesus.

"When you're in love with Jesus, you're going to love your wife more, you're going to love your husband more." – Mother Angelica

Hail Mary

"Blessed are the poor in spirit, for theirs is the Kingdom of heaven." (Matthew 5:3)

Holy Mother, I pray that I try every day to live a life of conversion, even if it's in small steps.

I am not only the Queen of Heaven but also the Mother of Mercy. – Our Mother to St. Sister Faustina

Hail Mary

Glory Be

Oh My Jesus (Fatima Prayer)

The Fourth Luminous Mystery
The Transfiguration

Lord, thank you for coming into this world as fully human so that we may form a personal relationship with You. May I never take Your teachings as mere guidance or philosophy from a learned teacher, but instead realize that these are the teachings of our Heavenly Father.

Our Father

"Truly I say to you, there are some standing here who will not taste death until they see the kingdom of God." (Luke 9:27)

Holy Mother, I rejoice that God so loved me that He humbled himself and became human.

"Everyone of us needs half an hour of prayer each day, except when we are busy – then we need an hour."
– St. Francis de Sales

Hail Mary

About eight days after He said this, He took Peter, John, and James and went up the mountain to pray.
(Luke 9:28)

Holy Mother, I pray that I take Jesus' words as God's Truth and not just the good advice of a scholar.

"No one can live continually in sin and continue to say the Rosary: either they will give up sin or they will give up the Rosary" – Bishop Hugh Doyle

Hail Mary

While He was praying His face changed in appearance and His clothing became dazzling white. (Luke 9:29)

Holy Mother, I pray that I make an effort to have a personal relationship with God since God tries to have a personal relationship with me through His son, Jesus Christ.

"When people love and recite the Rosary they find it makes them better." – St. Anthony Mary Claret

Hail Mary

And behold, two men were conversing with Him, Moses and Elijah, who appeared in glory and spoke of His exodus that He was going to accomplish in Jerusalem. (Luke 9:30-31)

Holy Mother, I pray for God's mercy on those who do not listen to Jesus' teaching.

"Never abandon prayer, even when it seems pointless to pray." – Pope Francis

Hail Mary

Peter and his companions had been overcome by sleep, but becoming fully awake, they saw His glory and the two men standing with Him. (Luke 9:32)

Holy Mother, I pray that I make time for Jesus to show himself to me in His glory through prayer and adoration.

"The family that prays together stays together."
– Fr. Patrick Peyton

Hail Mary

As they were about to part from Him, Peter said to Jesus, "Master, it is good that we are here; let us make three tents, one for You, one for Moses, and one for Elijah." (Luke 9:33)

Holy Mother, I pray that I make an effort to eliminate distractions in my life that prevent me from truly experiencing God's grace.

"The Rosary gradually gives us a perfect knowledge of Jesus Christ." – St. Louis de Montfort

Hail Mary

But he did not know what he was saying. (Luke 9:33)

Oh Lord, transfigure me through the Sacrament of Reconciliation from being bound by sin to free in Your grace.

"The Rosary purifies our souls, washing away sin."
– St. Louis de Montfort

Hail Mary

While he was still speaking, a cloud came and cast a shadow over them, and they became frightened when they entered the cloud. (Luke 9:34)

Holy Mother, I pray that I take the time to examine my conscious and see what areas of my life need to be transfigured from sin to grace.

"The Rosary gives us victory over all our enemies."
– St. Louis de Montfort

Hail Mary

Then from the cloud came a voice that said, "This is my chosen Son; listen to Him." (Luke 9:35)

Holy Mother, I pray that I honor Jesus with my every word, thought, and action.

"The Rosary makes it easy for us to practice virtue."
– St. Louis de Montfort

Hail Mary

After the voice had spoken, Jesus was found alone. They fell silent and did not at that time tell anyone what they had seen. (Luke 9:36)

Holy Mother, I pray that I not fear God's awesome power, but take comfort in His awesome capacity to love.

"The Rosary sets us on fire with love of Our Lord."
– St. Louis de Montfort

Hail Mary

Glory Be

Oh My Jesus (Fatima Prayer)

The Fifth Luminous Mystery
Institution of the Eucharist

Lord, increase my faith in Your true presence in the Holy Eucharist. May I never take the Eucharist for granted. May I have the awareness and humility not to receive You in an unworthy state of sin or with an unprepared heart.

Our Father

When the hour came, He took His place at table with the apostles. (Luke 22:14)

Holy Mother, I pray that I can look beyond what I can see and feel and have faith in the true presence of Christ in the Eucharist.

"Through the Rosary, sinners are forgiven."
– A blessing from the Rosary

Hail Mary

He said to them, "I have eagerly desired to eat this Passover with you before I suffer," (Luke 22:15)

Holy Mother, help me find comfort knowing that Jesus is physically present with us today in the Eucharist.

"Through the Rosary, souls that thirst are refreshed."
– A blessing from the Rosary

Hail Mary

"For, I tell you, I shall not eat it [again] until there is fulfillment in the kingdom of God." (Luke 22:16)

Holy Mother, I pray that I am properly prepared to receive the Eucharist by avoiding mortal sin and receiving the Sacrament of Reconciliation regularly.

"Through the Rosary, those who are fettered have their bonds broken." – A blessing from the Rosary

Hail Mary

Then He took a cup, gave thanks, and said, "Take this and share it among yourselves;" (Luke 22:17)

Holy Mother, I pray for mercy on those who receive the Eucharist with mortal sins on their souls.

"Through the Rosary, those who weep find happiness." – A blessing from the Rosary

Hail Mary

"For I tell you [that] from this time on I shall not drink of the fruit of the vine until the kingdom of God comes." (Luke 22:18)

Holy Mother, I pray that I look to the Eucharist for spiritual strength to endure life's challenges.

"Through the Rosary, those who are tempted find peace." – A blessing from the Rosary

Hail Mary

Then He took the bread, said the blessing, broke it, and gave it to them, saying, "This is my body, which will be given for you; do this in memory of me."
(Luke 22:19)

Holy Mother, I pray that I place all my faith that living by Jesus' teachings will lead me to His heavenly kingdom.

"Through the Rosary, the poor find help."
– A blessing from the Rosary

Hail Mary

And likewise the cup after they had eaten, saying, "This cup is the new covenant in my blood, which will be shed for you." (Luke 22:20)

Holy Mother, I pray for those who do not attend Mass without good reason on Sundays or holy days of obligation; that they receive God's forgiveness and return to His house.

"Through the Rosary, religious are reformed."
– A blessing from the Rosary

Hail Mary

"He who comes to me shall not hunger, and he who believes in me shall never thirst." (John 6:35)

Holy Mother, help me take the time to pray earnestly all through Mass, especially after receiving the Lord during Communion.

"Through the Rosary, those who are ignorant are instructed." – A blessing from the Rosary

Hail Mary

"He who eats my flesh and drinks my blood has life everlasting and I shall raise him up on the last day." (John 6:54)

Holy Mother, I pray for priests; that they internalize the faith that they profess and teach the truth of Jesus Christ

"Through the Rosary, the living learn to overcome pride." – A blessing from the Rosary

Hail Mary

"For my flesh is food indeed, and my blood is drink indeed" (John 6:56)

Holy Mother, I pray that I make time to be with Jesus through Eucharistic adoration.

"Through the Rosary, the dead (the Holy Souls) have their pains eased by suffrages."
– A blessing from the Rosary

Hail Mary

Glory Be

Oh My Jesus (Fatima Prayer)

The Sorrowful Mysteries

The Agony in the Garden

The Scourging

The Crowning of Thorns

Jesus Carries His Cross

The Crucifixion

The First Sorrowful Mystery
The Agony in the Garden

Lord, may hardship, sorrow, and distress pass over me. However, like Jesus, give me the strength to follow Your Will no matter where it may take me. May I remember that You never give anyone more challenges then he can handle.

Our Father

Then Jesus came with them to a place called Gethsemane, and He said to His disciples, "Sit here while I go over there and pray." (Matthew 26:36)

Heavenly Mother, I pray that I always make time for prayer as Jesus did in the Garden of Gesthemene.

"Where the Rosary is recited there will be peace and tranquility." – St. John Bosco

Hail Mary

He took along Peter and the two sons of Zebedee, and began to feel sorrow and distress. (Matthew 26:37)

Heavenly Mother, I pray that my prayers are focused and earnest, not mindless repetition.

"If He asks much of you it is because He knows you can give much." – St. Pope John Paul II

Hail Mary

Then He said to them, "My soul is sorrowful even to death. Remain here and keep watch with me." (Matthew 26:38)

Heavenly Mother, I pray for the faith and steadfastness not to give up prayer when times are tough.

"Being Marian is going to Heaven and hearing Jesus say, 'My mother told me everything about you.'"
– Unknown

Hail Mary

He advanced a little and fell prostrate in prayer, saying, "My Father, if it is possible, let this cup pass from me; yet, not as I will, but as You will."
(Matthew 26:39)

Heavenly Mother, I pray for trust in God's Will for me, even if I don't understand it or it is difficult to follow.

"In times of darkness, holding Rosary beads is like holding the Blessed Mother's hand." – Unknown

Hail Mary

When He returned to His disciples He found them asleep. He said to Peter, "So you could not keep watch with me for one hour? (Matthew 26:40)

Heavenly Mother, I pray for those who do not pray or believe in the fruitfulness of prayer.

"The Rosary is the Bible on a string."
– Fr. Ronan Murphy

Hail Mary

"Watch and pray that you may not undergo the test. The spirit is willing, but the flesh is weak."
(Matthew 26:41)

Heavenly Mother, I pray for the stillness of mind and body to listen to God through prayer.

"The Rosary catechizes using scripture."
– Fr. Ronan Murphy

Hail Mary

Withdrawing a second time, He prayed again, "My Father, if it is not possible that this cup pass without my drinking it, Your Will be done!" (Matthew 26:42)

Heavenly Mother, I pray for faith that God will see me through the difficult times in my life.

"The Rosary is the chain that binds Satan." – Fr. Gobbi

Hail Mary

Then He returned once more and found them asleep, for they could not keep their eyes open. (Matthew 26:43)

Heavenly Mother, help me have patience for God's plan for me to manifest itself.

"I have been all things unholy. If God can work through me, He can work through anyone."
– St. Francis of Assisi

Hail Mary

He left them and withdrew again and prayed a third time, saying the same thing again. (Matthew 26:44)

Heavenly Mother, I pray that God spares me difficulty in my life but, if not possible, that I find the strength to imitate Jesus by accepting God's Will.

"Oh God, forgive what I have been, correct what I am, and direct what I will be." – St. Elizabeth Ann Seton

Hail Mary

Then He returned to His disciples and said to them, "Are you still sleeping and taking your rest? Behold, the hour is at hand when the Son of Man is to be handed over to sinners. (Matthew 26:45)

Heavenly Mother, I pray that I make time for earnest prayer before Jesus in Eucharistic adoration.

"Love the Madonna and pray the Rosary, for Her Rosary is the weapon against the evils of today."
– St. Padre Pio

Hail Mary

Glory Be

Oh My Jesus (Fatima Prayer)

The Second Sorrowful Mystery
The Scourging at the Pillar

Lord, use me to comfort those who suffer. May those who suffer take comfort and hope for they follow in the footsteps of Jesus. And while they may not find relief in this world, may their faith in eternal happiness in Heaven give them strength.

Our Father

Then Pilate took Jesus and had Him scourged. (John 19:1)

Heavenly Mother, I pray for those who are suffering, whether it be minor inconveniences or serious persecution.

"The Rosary is a long chain that connects Heaven and Earth." – St. Therese of Lisieux

Hail Mary

Let us test him with insult and torture, that we may find out how gentle he is, and make trial of his forbearance. (Wisdom 2:19)

Heavenly Mother, I pray for those who suffer silently and do not think anyone cares about them.

"One end of the Rosary is in our hands and the other end is in the hands of the Holy Virgin."
– St. Therese of Lisieux

Hail Mary

But He was wounded for our transgressions, He was bruised for our iniquities: upon him was the chastisement that made us whole, and with his stripes we were healed. (Isaiah 53:5)

Heavenly Mother, I pray for those who suffer because of sinful choices; that they acknowledge their sins and seek God's forgiveness.

"The Rosary prayer rises like incense to the feet of the Almighty." – St. Therese of Lisieux

Hail Mary

Once more Pilate went out and said to them, "Look, I am bringing Him out to you, so that you may know that I find no guilt in Him." (John 19:4)

Heavenly Mother, I pray for the strength to endure any trials and hardship life brings.

"Mary responds at once like beneficial dew, bringing new life to human hearts." – St. Therese of Lisieux

Hail Mary

I am a man who has seen affliction under the rod of his wrath; he has driven and brought me into darkness without any light; surely against me he turns his hand again and again all the day long. (Lamentations 3:1-3)

Heavenly Mother, may the thought that we are all brothers and sisters in Christ prevent me from ever intentionally harming anyone.

"The Rosary is the best therapy for these distraught, unhappy, fearful and frustrated souls."
– Ven. Archbishop Fulton Sheen

Hail Mary

When the chief priests and the guards saw Him they cried out, "Crucify Him, crucify Him!" (John 19:6)

Heavenly Mother, I pray for mercy and the conversion of those who hate and persecute the Catholic Church.

"The Rosary involves the simultaneous use of three powers: the physical, the vocal, and the spiritual."
– Ven. Archbishop Fulton Sheen

Hail Mary

Pilate said to them, "Take Him yourselves and crucify Him. I find no guilt in Him." (John 19:6)

Heavenly Mother, help me fast and sacrifice for others in the name of my Lord, Jesus Christ.

"I want you to know that in this kind of warfare, the battering ram has always been the Rosary."
– Our Mother to St. Dominic

Hail Mary

The Jews answered, "We have a law, and according to that law He ought to die, because He made himself the Son of God." (John 19:7)

Heavenly Mother, help me find the strength to offer up my own sufferings to Jesus Christ.

"When you say the Rosary the angels rejoice, the Blessed Trinity delights, my Son finds joy, and I myself am happier than you can possibly guess."
– Our Mother to Blessed Alan de la Roche

Hail Mary

It was our infirmities that He bore, our sufferings, that He endured. (Isaiah 53:4)

Heavenly Mother, I pray that I realize just how much my sins pain Jesus and feel true sorrow for them.

"The Rosary isn't just a recitation of prayers, but a meditation on the grace of God." – www.catholic.com

Hail Mary

Upon Him was the chastisement that makes us whole, by His stripes we are healed. (Isaiah 53:5)

Heavenly Mother, help me be a source of comfort for those who suffer.

"Many come to see how Rosary meditations bring to mind the life and virtues not only of the Mother of God, but of Christ himself." – Unknown

Hail Mary

Glory Be

Oh My Jesus (Fatima Prayer)

The Third Sorrowful Mystery
The Crowning of Thorns

Lord, You were a most unexpected king crowned with thorns and scorn. May I recognize Your kingly presence in my life and honor You through love and charity.

Our Father

The soldiers led Him away inside the palace, that is, the praetorium, and assembled the whole cohort. (Mark 15:16)

Heavenly Mother, I pray for forgiveness for the times I have sinned and I did not give Jesus Christ the honor He deserves.

"The Rosary is the most beautiful and richest of all prayers to the Mediatrix of all grace." – St. Pope Pius X

Hail Mary

They clothed Him in purple and, weaving a crown of thorns, placed it on Him. (Mark 15:17)

Heavenly Mother, I pray for forgiveness for the times I have not recognized Jesus in my brothers and sisters.

"The Rosary is the prayer that touches most the heart of the Mother of God." – St. Pope Pius X

Hail Mary

They began to salute Him with, "Hail, King of the Jews!" (Mark 15:18)

Heavenly Mother, I pray for the desire to live in constant honor of Jesus by leading a life of prayer and charity.

"When prayed well in a truly meditative way, the Rosary leads to an encounter with Christ in His mysteries." – St. Pope John Paul II

Hail Mary

And kept striking His head with a reed and spitting upon Him. (Mark 15:19)

Heavenly Mother, I pray for the will to turn the world towards Jesus Christ by defending and proudly living the Catholic faith.

"If you are in danger, if your hearts are confused, turn to Mary. She is our comfort, our help."
– St. Francis Xavier Cabrini

Hail Mary

They knelt before Him in homage. (Mark 15:19)

Heavenly Mother, I pray that I do not take my faith for granted and always remember the precious gift that it is.

"Turn towards Her and you will be saved."
– St. Francis Xavier Cabrini

Hail Mary

And when they had mocked Him, they stripped Him of the purple cloak, dressed Him in His own clothes, and led Him out to crucify Him. (Mark 15:20)

Heavenly Mother, I pray in thanksgiving for the Lord Jesus suffering for my sake so that I may find eternal joy in Heaven.

"I want you to know that no one can please me more than by saying the Rosary." – Our Mother to St. Mechtilde

Hail Mary

Jesus therefore came forth, wearing the crown of thorns and the purple cloak. (John 19:5)

Heavenly Mother, I pray for mercy on those who live in mortal sin and for their conversion.

"Never will anyone who says his Rosary every day be led astray. This is a statement I would gladly sign with my blood." – St. Louis de Montfort

Hail Mary

For gold is tested in the fire, and acceptable men in the furnace of humiliation. (Sirach 2:5)

Heavenly Mother, I pray that I am aware of the evil Satan spreads in this world that mocks the Lord Jesus.

"How could I wear a crown of gold when my Lord wear a crown of thorns and He wears it for me?"
– St. Elizabeth of Hungary

Hail Mary

The greater you are, the more you must humble yourself, so that you will find favor in the sight of the Lord. (Sirach 3:19)

Heavenly Mother, I pray for awareness to help and comfort my brothers and sisters in Christ.

"The Rosary is the book of the simple, which initiates them into mysteries and knowledge more satisfying than the education of other men."
– Ven. Archbishop Fulton Sheen

Hail Mary

And, as one from whom men hide their faces, he was despised, and we esteemed him not. (Isaiah 53:3)

Heavenly Mother, I pray for those who suffer, that they find comfort in the fact that they imitate our Lord Jesus Christ.

"The Rosary is the book of the aged, whose eyes close up the shadow of this world, and open on the substance of the next." – Ven. Archbishop Fulton Sheen

Hail Mary

Glory Be

Oh My Jesus (Fatima Prayer)

The Fourth Sorrowful Mystery
The Carrying of the Cross

Lord, I know the road is long and hard. I may fall, either to sin or despair. But like You falling under the weight of the cross, may I always find the strength to get back up and follow God's Will.

Our Father

As they led Him away they took hold of a certain Simon, a Cyrenian, who was coming in from the country; (Luke 23:26)

Heavenly Mother, I pray for the strength to endure life's challenges by remaining faithful to the teachings of the Catholic Church.

"The power of the Rosary is beyond description."
– Ven. Archbishop Fulton Sheen

Hail Mary

And after laying the cross on him, they made him carry it behind Jesus. (Luke 23:26)

Heavenly Mother, help me find the will to help those who are burdened by difficulty and despair.

"When we feel our cross weighing upon us, let us have recourse to Mary, whom the Church calls the 'Consoler of the Afflicted.'"
– St. Alphonsus Maria de Liguori

Hail Mary

A large crowd of people followed Jesus, including many women who mourned and lamented Him. (Luke 23:27)

Heavenly Mother, I pray that I have hope and find peace despite life's challenges.

"Give yourself up into the arms of our Heavenly Mother. She will take good care of your soul."
– St. Padre Pio

Hail Mary

Jesus turned to them and said, "Daughters of Jerusalem, do not weep for me; weep instead for yourselves and for your children," (Luke 23:28)

Heavenly Mother, I pray for the comfort of those who live in despair and hopelessness.

"The Rosary is a sort of machine gun and atomic bomb, namely, a weapon that is far superior to all the weapons of modern warfare in overcoming the enemy of God." – Pope Leo XIII

Hail Mary

"For indeed, the days are coming when people will say, 'Blessed are the barren, the wombs that never bore and the breasts that never nursed.'" (Luke 23:29)

Heavenly Mother, I pray that I find the strength to receive the Sacrament of Reconciliation when I fall under the weight of sin.

"With this Rosary, I bend my children to the Immaculate Heart of Mary for Her guidance and protection." – Our Mother to Fr. Gobbi

Hail Mary

"At that time people will say to the mountains, 'Fall upon us!' and to the hills, 'Cover us!'" (Luke 23:30)

Heavenly Mother, I pray that I take up my cross as Jesus commanded and not hide from life's challenges.

"So your strength is failing you? Why don't you tell your mother about it?... Mother! Call Her with a loud voice." – St. Josemaria Escriva

Hail Mary

"For if these things are done when the wood is green what will happen when it is dry?" (Luke 23:31)

Heavenly Mother, help me understand that all of life's misfortunes are temporary and that I will find healing peace in God's heavenly kingdom.

"Mary is listening to you; She sees you in danger, perhaps and She, your Holy Mother Mary, offers you the refuge of Her arms and you will find yourself with added strength for the new battle." – St. Josemaria Escriva

Hail Mary

And bearing the cross for Himself, He went forth to the place called "The Skull." (John 19:17)

Heavenly Mother, I pray that I feel genuine sorrow for the sins I've committed and resolve to not commit them in the future.

"Take up your Rosary once again." – St. Pope John Paul II

Hail Mary

"Take My yoke upon you, and learn from Me."
(Matthew. 11:29)

Heavenly Mother, I pray for all the persecuted throughout the world; that they remain strong in their faith.

"A single "Blessed be God!" when things go wrong is of more value than a thousand acts of thanksgiving when things are to your liking." – St. John of Avila

Hail Mary

"And you will find rest for your souls. For my yoke is easy, and my burden light." (Matthew 11:29-30)

Heavenly Mother, help me take comfort that the Lord walks with us, even in our sufferings.

"It would be impossible to name all the many saints who discovered in the Rosary a genuine path to the growth of holiness." – St. Pope John Paul II

Hail Mary

Glory Be

Oh My Jesus (Fatima Prayer)

The Fifth Sorrowful Mystery
The Crucifixion

Lord, remember me and have mercy on me, a poor sinner. May I not receive what I rightly deserve through my imperfect life, but instead receive Your mercy so that I may live with You in Heaven.

Our Father

Then he handed Him over to them to be crucified. So they took Jesus, and carrying the cross himself He went out to what is called the Place of the Skull, in Hebrew, Golgotha. (John 19:17)

Heavenly Mother, I pray, that like the good criminal on the cross, I ask Jesus to simply remember me when I pray to Him.

"Anyone who goes to Mary and prays the Rosary cannot be touched by Satan." – Fr. Gabriel Amorth

Hail Mary

There they crucified Him, and with Him two others, one on either side, with Jesus in the middle.
(John 19:18)

Heavenly Mother, I pray that I show faith in God's plan instead of asking Him to "prove himself" to me like some of the people who witnessed Him on the cross.

"I know a thousand psychoanalysts who will explain sins away, but that is not what we want. We want them forgiven." – Ven. Archbishop Fulton Sheen

Hail Mary

Pilate also had an inscription written and put on the cross. It read, "Jesus the Nazorean, the King of the Jews." (John 19:19)

Heavenly Mother, I pray that I express hope even in the darkest moments in my life.

"Rediscover the Rosary in the light of scripture, in harmony with the liturgy, and in the context of your daily lives." – St. Pope John Paul II

Hail Mary

Now many of the Jews read this inscription, because the place where Jesus was crucified was near the city; and it was written in Hebrew, Latin, and Greek. (John 19:20)

Heavenly Mother, I pray for strength to imitate Jesus by offering my sufferings for the benefit of others.

"Let us highly esteem devotion to the Blessed Virgin, and let us lose no opportunity of inspiring others with it." – St. Alphonsus Liguori

Hail Mary

Standing by the cross of Jesus were His mother and His mother's sister, Mary the wife of Clopas, and Mary of Magdala. (John 19:25)

Heavenly Mother, I pray that I show love and forgiveness to those who hurt me.

"Mary seeks for those who approach Her devoutly and with reverence, for such She loves, nourishes, and adopts as Her children."– St. Bonaventure

Hail Mary

When Jesus saw His mother and the disciple there whom He loved, He said to His mother, "Woman, behold, Your son." (John 19:26)

Heavenly Mother, I pray for the peace and conversion of all those consumed by hatred and jealousy.

"If anyone does not wish to have Mary Immaculate for his mother, he will not have Christ for his brother."
– St. Maximilian Kolbe

Hail Mary

Then He said to the disciple, "Behold, your mother." And from that hour the disciple took Her into his home. (John 19:27)

Heavenly Mother, I pray for those who have been treated unfairly, that they find peace and comfort; if not in this life, may they take comfort that they will find it in Heaven.

"Tell everyone that God grants graces through the Immaculate Heart of Mary." – St. Jacinta Marto

Hail Mary

After this, aware that everything was now finished, in order that the scripture might be fulfilled, Jesus said, "I thirst." (John 19:28)

Heavenly Mother, I pray for the forgiveness of those who persecute Jesus' Church for "they know not what they do."

"Jesus himself did not try to convert the two thieves on the cross; He waited until one of them turned to Him."
– Dietrich Bonhoeffer

Hail Mary

There was a vessel filled with common wine. So they put a sponge soaked in wine on a sprig of hyssop and put it up to His mouth. (John 19:29)

Heavenly Mother, I pray that I see the face of Jesus in those around me who suffer and be moved by compassion to help them.

"There is no surer road to Jesus than the one through Mary." – St. Louis de Montfort

Hail Mary

When Jesus had taken the wine, He said, "It is finished." And bowing His head, He handed over the spirit. (John 19:30)

Heavenly Mother, help me have the strength to stand with the Church even among persecution.

"Do not be ashamed to recite the Rosary alone, while you walk along the streets to school, to the university, or to work, or as you commute by public transport."
– St. Pope John Paul II

Hail Mary

Glory Be

Oh My Jesus (Fatima Prayer)

The Glorious Mysteries

The Resurrection

The Ascension

Pentecost

The Assumption

The Coronation of Mary

The First Glorious Mystery
The Resurrection

Lord, as You promised, You rose from the dead. You always kept Your promises which means I must embrace the cross as You instructed if I am to rise to a new life in You. Grant me the strength to live for Your kingdom that You opened up to all of humanity when You rose from the dead.

Our Father

After the Sabbath, as the first day of the week was dawning, Mary Magdalene and the other Mary came to see the tomb. (Matthew: 28:1)

Heavenly Queen, help me to live towards one day living in the Kingdom of Heaven and not solely for my earthly desires.

"The Rosary is the book of the blind, where souls see and there enact the greatest drama of love the world has ever known." – Ven. Archbishop Fulton Sheen

Hail Mary

And behold, there was a great earthquake; for an angel of the Lord descended from heaven, approached, rolled back the stone, and sat upon it. (Matthew: 28:2)

Heavenly Queen, help me accept that Jesus' teachings, as taught by the Catholic Church, are God's truth.

"Sacrifice yourselves for sinners and say often, especially when you make some sacrifice, 'Jesus, this is for the love of You, for the conversion of sinners, and in reparation for the offenses committed against the Immaculate Heart of Mary.'"
– Our Mother to the children of Fatima

Hail Mary

His appearance was like lightning and His clothing was white as snow. (Matthew: 28:3)

Heavenly Queen, I pray that I live with joy in a risen Christ who opened the gates of Heaven for all those in the world.

"Pray a great deal and make many sacrifices, for many souls go to Hell because they have no one to make sacrifices and to pray for them."
– Our Mother to the children of Fatima

Hail Mary

The guards were shaken with fear of Him and became like dead men. (Matthew: 28:4)

Heavenly Queen, I pray that You instill a sense of hope in those who do not live in the joy of the Resurrection but in a state of hopelessness.

"Say the Rosary every day to obtain peace for the world." – Our Mother to the children of Fatima

Hail Mary

Then the angel said to the women in reply, "Do not be afraid! I know that you are seeking Jesus the crucified. (Matthew: 28:5)

Heavenly Queen, I pray that I may help others see the joy and triumph of the Catholic faith over sin and death.

"Let no one ever come to you without leaving better and happier." – St. Mother Teresa

Hail Mary

He is not here, for He has been raised just as He said. Come and see the place where He lay. (Matthew: 28:6)

Heavenly Queen, I pray that by believing in the resurrection, my faith in all of Jesus' teachings is strengthened.

"Be the living expression of God's kindness."
– St. Mother Teresa

Hail Mary

Then go quickly and tell His disciples, 'He has been raised from the dead, and He is going before you to Galilee; there you will see Him.' Behold, I have told you." (Matthew: 28:7)

Heavenly Queen, I pray for those who suffer, that they may see hope in their lives through your Son's resurrection.

"All the devils venerate and fear the name Mary to such a degree, that on hearing it they immediately loosen the claws with which they hold the soul captive." – St. Bridget

Hail Mary

Then they went away quickly from the tomb, fearful yet overjoyed, and ran to announce this to His disciples. (Matthew: 28:8)

Heavenly Queen, help me meditate on the grace of the risen Christ when I receive Him in the Eucharist.

"You wish to reform the world? Reform yourself, otherwise your efforts will be in vain."
– St. Ignatius Loyola

Hail Mary

And behold, Jesus met them on their way and greeted them. They approached, embraced His feet, and did Him homage. (Matthew: 28:9)

Heavenly Queen, help me focus on my own spiritual resurrection when I will stand before God in His Heavenly Kingdom.

"When the devil wishes to make himself master of a soul, he seeks to make it give up devotion to Mary."
– St. Alphonsus Liguori

Hail Mary

Then Jesus said to them, "Do not be afraid. Go tell my brothers to go to Galilee, and there they will see me." (Matthew: 28:10)

Heavenly Queen, I pray that I look forward to appreciating the fullness of Jesus' resurrection when I enter God's Heavenly Kingdom.

"Let us highly esteem devotion to the Blessed Virgin, and let us lose no opportunity of inspiring others with it." – St. Alphonsus Liguori

Hail Mary

Glory Be

Oh My Jesus (Fatima Prayer)

The Second Glorious Mystery
The Ascension

Lord, You ascended into Your Kingdom where You sit at the right hand of God. Have mercy on all those who come before You for judgment. You left this world leaving Your Church in my hands. Grant me the strength to act as a good steward of Your teachings.

Our Father

And He said to them, "Thus it is written that the Messiah would suffer and rise from the dead on the third day" (Luke 24:46)

Heavenly Queen, help me faithfully continue Christ's mission of love and healing.

"O noble Virgin, truly You are greater than any other greatness... for You are God's place of repose."
– St. Athanasius

Hail Mary

"And that repentance, for the forgiveness of sins, would be preached in His name to all the nations, beginning from Jerusalem. (Luke 24:47)

Heavenly Queen, I pray for mercy on those who have died and face Jesus at the right hand of the Father for judgment.

"A joyless Catholic is the devil's best tool."
– Scott Hahn

Hail Mary

"You are witnesses of these things. And [behold] I am sending the promise of my Father upon you;"
(Luke 24:48-49)

Heavenly Queen, I pray for the conversion of those who do not accept the reality of Christ as our ultimate judge.

"A joyful Catholic is God's greatest instrument."
– Scott Hahn

Hail Mary

"But stay in the city until you are clothed with power from on high." (Luke 24:49)

Heavenly Queen, I pray for forgiveness for those times I have not been a living witness to the Catholic faith.

"I really only love God as much as I love the person I love least." – Dorothy Day

Hail Mary

Then He led them [out] as far as Bethany, raised His hands, and blessed them. (Luke 24:50)

Heavenly Queen, I pray that I may find the time to receive the Sacrament of Reconciliation so I can live in God's grace.

"Prayer is powerful beyond limits when we turn to the Immaculate who is queen even of God's heart."
– St. Maximilian Kolbe

Hail Mary

As He blessed them He parted from them and was taken up to heaven. (Luke 24:51)

Heavenly Queen, I pray for the faith that Jesus in Heaven hears and answers my prayers.

"There is no surer means of calling down God's blessings upon the family than the daily recitation of the Rosary." – Pope Pius XII

Hail Mary

They did Him homage and then returned to Jerusalem with great joy, and they were continually in the temple praising God. (Luke 24:52-53)

Heavenly Queen, I pray that I follow the teachings of the Church started by the disciples who witnessed Jesus' ascension.

"God is not a God of the emotions but the God of truth." – Dietrich Bonhoeffer

Hail Mary

"Go, therefore, and make disciples of all nations."
(Matthew 28:19)

Heavenly Queen, I pray for faith to believe that Jesus is still with us physically in the Eucharist.

"You can't pray a ten cent prayer and expect a million dollar answer." –Unknown

Hail Mary

"Teaching them to observe all that I have commanded you." (Matthew 28:20)

Heavenly Queen, I pray for all those who suffer loss, that they find comfort in Jesus who is forever with us in His Heavenly Kingdom.

"Give me an army saying the Rosary and I will conquer the world." – Blessed Pope Pius IX

Hail Mary

"He who believes and is baptized shall be saved."
(Mark 16:16)

Heavenly Queen, I pray that I rejoice in Jesus taking our humanity with Him into Heaven to prepare a place for me.

"Keep the joy of loving God in your heart and share this joy with all you meet." – St. Mother Teresa

Hail Mary

Glory Be

Oh My Jesus (Fatima Prayer)

The Third Glorious Mystery
Pentecost

Lord, grant me the humility to submit my will to the Holy Spirit. May I understand that Your Will, no matter how challenging or ridiculous it may seem, is the only way to eternal joy in Heaven.

Our Father

"And I will ask the Father, and He will give you another Advocate to be with you always, the Spirit of truth, which the world cannot accept, because it neither sees nor knows it." (John 14:16-17)

Heavenly Queen, I pray that I let the Holy Spirit guide my actions.

"Our Lady has never refused me a grace through the recitation of the Rosary." – St. Padre Pio

Hail Mary

"But you know it, because it remains with you, and will be in you. I will not leave you orphans;" (John 14:17-18)

Heavenly Queen, I pray that I actively try to hear the Holy Spirit in the calmness of prayer.

"True love comes from God and is expressed through His mercy and forgiveness." – Pope Francis

Hail Mary

"I will come to you. In a little while the world will no longer see me, but you will see me, because I live and you will live." (John 14:19)

Heavenly Queen, I pray for the courage to trust the Holy Spirit even if He leads me down a difficult road.

"Evil draws its power from indecision and concern for what other people think." – Pope Benedict XVI

Hail Mary

"On that day you will realize that I am in my Father and you are in me and I in you." (John 14:20)

Heavenly Queen, I pray for those with a hardened heart, that they let the Holy Spirit into their hearts to transform them into lovers of Christ.

"The final battle between the Lord and the reign of Satan will be about marriage and the family. Don't be afraid... this is the decisive issue." – St. Lucia of Fatima

Hail Mary

"Whoever has my commandments and observes them is the one who loves me. And whoever loves me will be loved by my Father, and I will love him and reveal myself to him." (John 14:21)

Heavenly Queen, I pray for priests everywhere, that they are led by the Holy Spirit to accurately teach God's Word.

"Take courage and pray; your guardian angel will also pray for you, and your prayers will be answered."
– St. Josemaria Escriva

Hail Mary

Judas, not the Iscariot, said to Him, "Master, [then] what happened that You will reveal Yourself to us and not to the world?" (John 14:22)

Heavenly Queen, I pray for the newly baptized and confirmed, that they take full advantage of God's grace poured onto them in the sacraments.

"It is impossible to find a saint who did not take the "two P's" seriously: Prayer and Penance."
– St. Francis Xavier Cabrini

Hail Mary

Jesus answered and said to him, "Whoever loves me will keep my word, and my Father will love him, and we will come to him and make our dwelling with him." (John 14:23)

Heavenly Queen, I pray that I do not fear the often hostile world for I know God guides me through the Holy Spirit.

"The Rosary is a school of prayer, the Rosary is a school of faith!" – Pope Francis

Hail Mary

"Whoever does not love me does not keep my words; yet the word you hear is not mine but that of the Father who sent me." (John 14:24)

Heavenly Queen, help me take advantage of the power of the Holy Spirit to forgive sins by regularly receiving the Sacrament of Reconciliation.

"Never abandon prayer, even when it seems pointless to pray." – Pope Francis

Hail Mary

"I have told you this while I am with you. The Advocate, the Holy Spirit that the Father will send in my name—He will teach you everything and remind you of all that I told you." (John 14:25-26)

Heavenly Queen, I pray that I take comfort knowing Your Son did not abandon this world but continues to guide us through the Holy Spirit.

"You are the gate through which all find Jesus."
– St. Alphonsus Liguori

Hail Mary

Wisdom from above is first of all pure, then peaceable, gentle, open to reason, full of mercy and good fruits. (James 3:17)

Heavenly Queen, I pray for the humility to acknowledge that my skills and talents are bestowed on me by the Holy Spirit.

"You can fly to Heaven on the wings of Confession and Communion." – St. John Bosco

Hail Mary

Glory Be

Oh My Jesus (Fatima Prayer)

The Fourth Glorious Mystery
The Assumption

Lord, You chose Mary to bring You into this world and hence She is the mother of all the faithful. May I listen to the guidance of the Holy Mother who only wants what is best for me – to one day join the angels and saints in Your Heavenly Kingdom.

Our Father

"Blessed are you who believed that what was spoken to you by the Lord would be fulfilled." (Luke 1:45)

Heavenly Queen, I pray that I make time to pray regularly and ask for Your intercession.

"The Rosary is the scourge of the devil."
– Pope Adrian VI

Hail Mary

And Mary said: "My soul proclaims the greatness of the Lord; my spirit rejoices in God my savior." (Luke 1:46-47)

Heavenly Queen, help me read the scriptures as well as Church documents to learn and love the Catholic faith.

"The Rosary is my favorite prayer. A marvelous prayer! Marvelous in its simplicity and depth."
– St. Pope John Paul II

Hail Mary

"For He has looked upon His handmaid's lowliness; behold, from now on will all ages call me blessed." (Luke 1:48)

Heavenly Queen, I pray that I make an effort to fast and offer my sacrifices to God.

"If you desire peace in your hearts, in your homes, and in your country, recite the Rosary." – Pope Pius XI

Hail Mary

In every nation which shall hear thy name, the God of Israel shall be magnified on occasion of thee. (Judith 13:31)

Heavenly Queen, I pray that I make time to receive the Sacrament of Confession to fully live in God's grace.

"Among all the devotions approved by the Church none has been so favored by so many miracles as the devotion of the Most Holy Rosary" – Pope Pius IX

Hail Mary

Hear, O daughter, and see; turn your ear, for the king shall desire your beauty. (Psalms 44:11-1 2)

Heavenly Queen, I pray that I receive the Eucharist with a worthy soul free of mortal sin.

"The greatest method of praying is to pray the Rosary." – St. Francis de Sales

Hail Mary

And the temple of God in heaven was opened, and there came flashes of lightning, and peals of thunder. (Revelations 11:19)

Heavenly Queen, I pray for the spiritual awakening of those who do not pray.

"…if you wish peace to reign in your homes, recite the family Rosary." – Pope St. Pius X

Hail Mary

And a great sign appeared in heaven: a woman clothed with the sun. (Revelations 12:1)

Heavenly Queen, I pray that You instill the desire to grow closer to God in those who have not learned their faith.

"From Mary, we learn to trust even when all hope seems gone." – St. Pope John Paul II

Hail Mary

And the moon was under Her feet, and upon Her head a crown of twelve stars. (Revelations 12:1)

Heavenly Queen, I pray for forgiveness for those times I have overindulged in earthly desires leaving no room for spiritual needs.

"The throne of Mary is so intimately connected with the throne and glory of Jesus that to deny the one is at the same time a denial of the other."
– Blessed William Joseph Chaminade

Hail Mary

All glorious is the king's daughter as she enters; her raiment is threaded with spun gold. (Psalms 44:14)

Heavenly Queen, I pray for those who have not received the Sacrament of Reconciliation in a long time; that they find the courage to humbly ask for God's forgiveness.

"Abandon yourself into the hands of Mary. She will take care of you." – St. Padre Pio

Hail Mary

Sing to the Lord a new song, for He has done wondrous deeds. (Psalms 97:1)

Heavenly Queen, I pray for mercy on those who do not regularly receive the Eucharist or receive it in an unworthy state.

"If you can't feed a hundred people, then feed just one." – St. Mother Teresa

Hail Mary

Glory Be

Oh My Jesus (Fatima Prayer)

The Fifth Glorious Mystery
The Coronation of Mary

Lord, I ask Mary, our Heavenly Mother, for Her protection from evil and temptation. I ask the Queen of Angels to send guardians from the Heavenly Hosts to watch and protect me.

Our Father

The Mighty One has done great things for me, and holy is His name. (Luke 1:49)

Heavenly Queen, thank you for the protection you and my guardian angels provide me.

"No one reaches the kingdom of Heaven except by humility." – St. Augustine

Hail Mary

His mercy is from age to age to those who fear Him. (Luke 1:50)

Heavenly Queen, I pray for Your protection against evil.

"He who loves the Immaculate will gain a sure victory in the interior combat." – St. Maximilian Kolbe

Hail Mary

He has shown might with His arm, dispersed the arrogant of mind and heart. (Luke 1:51)

Heavenly Queen, I pray for an inner peace by accepting God's Will.

"If God sends you many sufferings, it is a sign that He has great plans for you and certainly wants to make you a saint." – St. Ignatius Loyola

Hail Mary

He has thrown down the rulers from their thrones but lifted up the lowly. (Luke 1:52)

Heavenly Queen, bring me closer to Your son, Jesus Christ.

"The Church exists in order to communicate precisely this: Truth, Beauty, and Goodness in person."
– Pope Francis

Hail Mary

The hungry He has filled with good things; the rich He has sent away empty. (Luke 1:53)

Heavenly Queen, I pray that I look to You to amplify and clarify my intentions.

"What does it take to become a saint? Will it."
– St. Thomas Aquinas

Hail Mary

He has helped Israel His servant, remembering His mercy, according to His promise to our fathers, to Abraham and to His descendants forever."
(Luke 1:54-55)

Heavenly Queen, help me better understand the will of Your son, Jesus Christ.

"The things you take for granted someone else is praying for." – Marlan Rico Lee

Hail Mary

I am the mother of fair love, and of fear, and of knowledge, and of holy hope. (Sirach 24:24)

Heavenly Queen, I pray for peace in our world starting with an understanding and desire of what I can do personally.

"Since our souls will be eternal, we ought to procure not a fortune that soon ends, but one that will be everlasting." – St. Alphonsus Liguori

Hail Mary

In me is all grace of the way and of truth, in me is all hope of life and of virtue. (Sirach 24:25)

Heavenly Queen, I pray that I strive to imitate You in living a pure and faithful life.

"The smallest thing, when done for the love of God, is priceless." – St. Teresa of Avila

Hail Mary

Come to me, all you that yearn for me, and be filled with my fruits. (Sirach 24:26)

Heavenly Queen, help me show humility like You and, in doing so, be raised up in God's grace.

"She who is the Mother of Sorrows and also the Mother of Consolation can understand you completely and help you." – St. Pope John Paul II

Hail Mary

So now, children, listen to me; instruction and wisdom do not reject! (Proverbs 8:32-33)

Heavenly Queen, I pray that I have the foresight to turn to You when facing any of life's difficulties.

"Don't spend your energies on things that generate worry, anxiety, and anguish. Only one thing is necessary: lift up your spirit and love God."
– St. Padre Pio

Hail Mary

Glory Be

Oh My Jesus (Fatima Prayer)

ABOUT THE AUTHOR

Brent Villalobos created www.rosarymeds.com in 2008. It is a website dedicated to helping people better understand and appreciate the Rosary and integrate Rosary prayer into their daily lives. Through various articles, the site makes connections between the themes of the Rosary, scripture, and current events to show what the Rosary can teach us about better living by forging a deeper relationship with God. In addition to the RosaryMeds website, Brent wrote *The Rosary for the Rest of Us;* a book that explains in a very plain way the main themes and ideas of each Rosary mystery.

Made in the USA
Middletown, DE
21 December 2020